Caring For Your Dog

by Mark McPherson

photography by
Marianne Bernstein

Troll Associates

Library of Congress Cataloging in Publication Data

McPherson, Mark (Mark D.)
  Caring for your dog.

  Includes index.
  Summary: An illustrated guide to caring for and
raising a puppy as a pet. Includes information on
selection, feeding, grooming, housebreaking, and
training.
  1. Dogs—Juvenile literature. [1. Dogs]
I. Bernstein, Marianne, ill. II. Title.
SF426.5.M33   1984   636.7   84-222
ISBN 0-8167-0113-X (lib. bdg.)
ISBN 0-8167-0114-8 (pbk.)

The author and publisher wish to thank the Animal Medical Center and the ASPCA of New York City, Akitas of Distinction, and Laura and
Alexander Spellman.

Photographs on pages 5, 7, and 10 by Aaron Norman.

10   9   8   7   6   5   4   3   2   1

Contents

Finding the Right Puppy

Few things in life will excite you and please you more than your first puppy. A puppy will draw out your warmest affections. Its cute and frisky behavior will inspire many hours of fun and laughter. Bold yet helpless, proud yet shy, a new puppy will depend on you for love, care, discipline, and training.

Selecting the right puppy is the first important step.

There are many things to consider before you select your puppy. For instance, how big a dog do you want? Do you want one as small as a Scottish Terrier or as large as a Great Dane? Or are you thinking of one that is somewhere in between?

This mixed-breed pup is part Pekingese, and part Lhasa Apso.

The large paws of this German shepherd puppy provide a hint of how big he will be when he is fully grown.

You also have to decide whether you want to get a purebred or a mixed breed. A purebred is a dog with parents that are both of the same breed, or type, such as two collies or two beagles. A mixed breed is a cross between at least two different types of dogs. An example of a mixed breed might be a dog whose father is a collie and whose mother is a German shepherd. A mixed breed can also be the result of parents that are themselves mixed breeds.

Do you want a dog with long or short hair? Dogs with long hair tend to shed more hair and also need frequent brushing.

The most important thing to do before you get your puppy is to have a talk with your parents. They will want to know whether you are ready to take on the responsibility of owning a dog. And they can advise you on whether the kind of dog you want is the best one for you, for them, and for your home.

Every puppy is cute, but cuteness is no

guarantee that a puppy will be a good pet. If you want to own a puppy that will grow up to be a good dog, don't select the first helpless little pup that you meet.

Many puppies get off to such a bad start —they are not treated kindly enough or given the proper nutrition or attention—that they will not grow up to be good pets. This is why you should look at, and compare, puppies from at least two separate litters (a litter is a recently born family of puppies). The same rule applies if you want to buy a purebred dog directly from a dog breeder. Visit at least two breeders so that you can make a comparison and select the best available puppy.

How do you find the right puppy for you? The first thing to do is to check bulletin boards and newspapers for notices announcing new puppies. Most people whose dogs have puppies are anxious to find good homes for the little ones, so they often give the pups away.

A long-haired dog like this beautiful Afghan hound requires a lot of brushing.

The eager, friendly nature of the Siberian husky has made it a favorite choice for a pet.

Call these people before you visit them. Ask how old the pups are and when you can stop by to look at them. Puppies should not leave their mothers until they are about two months old. The best time for you to see them is a couple of weeks before, when they are about six weeks old.

There are several things to look for when you select a puppy. First, the mother dog should be well-behaved, calm, and attentive. A nervous or timid mother is likely to have nervous and timid pups. A good mother will be friendly to you, watchful over her litter, and in good health.

Second, the pups should be plump and clean and have shiny coats. They should have bright eyes that are not runny. Pups should not have a bad smell or smelly ears. Don't start out with an unhealthy pup. All puppies need shots, and many will have to be treated for worms. Those things are normal. But general good health should be apparent.

Third, it is important that the people who own the litter should have handled the pups early and often. Pups who get used to being handled by people at an early age are already on the road toward getting along well with people.

Fourth, how does each individual pup react to you? Handle each one gently and carefully. A friendly and healthy pup will enjoy the attention. Take the pup off to the side and put him on the floor. Get on your knees and gently slap your hands together in front of you. A pup that comes right to you, eager to play and sniff, will make a good pet. This dog is on its way to getting along well with people. A pup that trem-

Hunting dogs like this English pointer sometimes become nervous if they always have to stay inside. It would be a good pet for you if you live in the country and can spend a lot of time with your dog outdoors.

bles and shudders, or rolls right over onto its back, is not off to a good start. He may never get along well with people.

Fifth, you should have good feelings about the pup. Do you like his color? How does the pup's personality affect you? If the pup checks out well in all of the other categories, make sure that he is also pleasing to you. This may be the most important point of all!

All of these things contribute to a good start. They do not guarantee that you will have a perfect pet. But when you get the pup home and begin training and caring for him, you will understand how important a good start is!

Often, people want to own a particular kind of dog, one that is a "pure breed." It is rare for families with purebred puppies to give them away for free. Usually you must pay for them. But you can always check to see what is available by reading the newspapers. The advantage of a pure-bred is that you will know more about what the puppy will be like as an adult, both in size and temperament.

Different breeds of dogs are bred for different reasons. Some are bred for hunting or for herding such animals as cows and sheep. Others are bred to be guard dogs. Most can be turned into good pets, but you must be careful. A dog bred and trained as a hunting dog, for example, is not necessarily going to make a good house pet. Such a dog may be loyal and obedient, but because he has been raised to hunt, being indoors much of the time may make the dog nervous.

The best advice on purebreds is to go directly to a professional breeder who raises the type of dogs you're interested in. Dogs sold directly by breeders usually receive more careful attention

This pug, a purebred, looks like it has a sad face.

than those sold through pet stores. When you meet the young purebred pups, judge them by the same standards you would use for the mixed breeds. Don't be overwhelmed by the atmosphere of a professional kennel. Concentrate on getting the right dog for you.

The American Kennel Club has information about different breeders in your area. When you buy a dog from a professional breeder, be sure that it has already been checked by a veterinarian (a pet doctor), and find out which shots it has had and which are still needed.

A good place to find a mixed-breed dog is the animal shelter. But you must be careful. Many of these animals are unwanted or abandoned. If they are older than six months, these dogs may have been made unfriendly by a lack of loving care. But most of these puppies will make fine pets.

Shelters should allow you to "interview" several dogs *outside* their cages. Take advantage of this opportunity to find a dog that is healthy, friendly, and relatively calm. If it is an older dog it should be obedient to basic commands like "sit" and "stay."

Before you choose your dog, you must make one important decision. Do you want a male, a female, or does it not make any difference? Male dogs are more likely to run away, and they may get into more fights than females. A vet can "neuter" a male dog so that this is less likely to occur.

Female dogs, on the other hand, can go into "heat." This means that they are ready to have puppies and will attract male dogs. A vet can "spay" a female dog so that she can't have pups.

Female dogs are sometimes a little more easy-going than males. But both male and female dogs can make good pets. You may just decide to take home the best-looking and most intelligent puppy you meet, regardless of its sex.

If you have decided to raise a puppy (rather than take in an older dog), you should prepare ahead of time for its arrival. You can bring the pup home when it is two months (or eight weeks) old. You have done your best to choose a physically and psychologically healthy pup. Now begins the year-long task of training your pup to be a wonderful pet.

Your new puppy will need lots of gentle handling to make it feel at home.

2

Bringing Your Puppy Home

Both you and your puppy will never have a harder time than your first few days together. The pup will be so upset at being separated from his mother and brothers and sisters that you may wonder if you made the right choice. The pup will be sad. He will cry during the night. He will even seem to reject your affection. Be patient. Think about how you would feel being separated from your family for the first time.

This little fellow moved right into his padded box. Nearby are two bowls, one for food and one for water. Newspapers keep his messes off the floor, and a leash keeps him near the newspapers when he starts to roam around.

13

The first thing to do for your pup is to have its corner ready. The young puppy needs a bed, which can be made with a cut-down cardboard box and an old towel laid across the bottom. Cover the floor around the box with newspapers. The newspapers will be the puppy's bathroom, until he learns to go outside.

The puppy also needs two bowls, one for food and one for water. Always keep the water bowl filled with fresh water. You must also have a leash and two collars—a regular leather collar for normal wear and a chain slip collar for training. Buy the collars after you get the puppy.

A new puppy cannot be allowed to roam freely. Most of the time you must keep a new pup leashed in his corner so that his frequent messes will be contained to one area. Tie the leash to a hook a couple of feet above the pup's head so that puppy and leash won't get tangled together. Another way to confine the puppy is to build barricades around his corner.

To fix your puppy a meal, pour puppy chow into the bowl, moisten it with warm water, and add a heaping tablespoon of canned dog food.

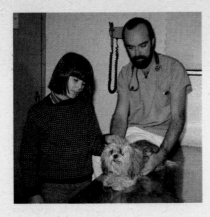

Take your new dog to see the veterinarian within a week after you bring it home.

Your puppy will want to eat three, sometimes four times a day. Ask the original owner what kind of food the puppy got, so you can feed the same kind, at least for the first week or so. Buy the specially prepared puppy food sold in stores. Soften this with a little warm water and add in a heaping tablespoon of canned dog food. This mixture will supply the nutrition your puppy needs. Do not give the puppy table scraps either now or when he is grown up. Gradually decrease the number of meals per day as the pup grows older. After he is a year old, he will need only one meal a day of dry adult dog food mixed with canned dog food.

What should you do if a new puppy cries and yelps all night long? Two remedies often work. Try both of them together. The first is to wrap a hot-water bottle in a towel and place it in the puppy's bed. The second is to wrap a ticking clock in a piece of cloth and place it next to the hot-water bottle. These will remind the puppy of the warmth and the heartbeat of his mother. If these fail, the only thing that will help is patience. The puppy will calm down, probably before a week has passed.

Sometime during the first week, you and your parents should take the puppy to the vet for an examination and for whatever shots he needs. Even if the pup has already had the first round of shots, take him to the vet anyway for the checkup. Ask the vet any questions you might have about the puppy's health.

Remember that most cities and towns require that you license your pup between the ages of three and six months.

As your puppy gets used to his new home, you will find that he has more energy than you thought possible. He will poke into everything, follow everybody, and be incredibly lovable. Now, after his initial period of sadness has passed, is the time to begin earning your puppy's love, loyalty, and obedience.

A big part of your job as owner of a new puppy is to walk it at least four or five times a day. The young dog has to get used to going to the bathroom outdoors.

Always be gentle with your puppy. Pet him affectionately, to calm him and to show your love. Learn how to pick up the puppy properly.

Most important of all, begin to teach him that he must go to the bathroom outdoors. This is a long, often difficult job, so it is best to get started early.

16

3

Housebreaking

To make housebreaking a puppy less difficult, you must have patience. Puppies are smart, but they aren't that smart. If you are lucky, it will take only until the puppy is six months old to finish teaching him to go to the bathroom outdoors. You should begin to get results after two weeks, but the pup will continue to make mistakes for a few months. In an extremely difficult case, it can take until the pup is a year old.

Begin the process during the very first

When your puppy goes to the bathroom out-doors, praise him so that he knows he has been good.

week you have your puppy. Puppies go to the bathroom frequently, and where they please. They usually want to go right after they eat. So, after your pup finishes each of his daily meals, wait a minute or two and then carry him outside. Take him to the same place every time. This will begin to get the idea across.

In addition to a walk after each meal, take the puppy out early in the morning (get up earlier than usual) and before you go to bed at night. That adds up to at least six walks a day, at first. It is even a good idea to take the puppy out a few more times in between meals. Whenever the puppy goes to the bathroom outside, praise him as though he had just won a gold medal. Make the puppy feel proud of his accomplishment.

During his early days in your home your puppy will make most of his messes on the news-

When your puppy messes indoors, scold him—but only if you catch him in the act.

papers, which should cover the entire area he can reach while tied to the leash. The newspapers are there as a convenience for you. As soon as you find a mess on them, wrap them up, put them in a plastic bag, and put that with the garbage outside. Then put down a fresh layer of newspapers.

Once you decide to let the pup roam freely in the house, don't bother trying to train him to use the newspaper. That is a wasted step. Treat messes made on the newspaper just as you would those made elsewhere. Watch the pup carefully as he explores a room. Learn the tell-tale signs that indicate his need to go to the bathroom. For example, he will probably sniff around the floor and try to find a private place. When the puppy does these things, pick him up and take him right outside.

If you get the puppy outside in time, pet, pat, and praise him as soon as he is finished.

If the pup *does* mess on the floor or the rug, you must catch him during, or only a few seconds after, the act. Only under these conditions should you discipline the pup. Grab him by the fur on the back of his neck, show the pup the mess, and say "No" in a loud voice. Shake the puppy a little so that he gets a sense that this is wrong. Then take him outside so that he gets a sense of the *right* place to make a mess.

Don't rub the puppy's face in a mess, don't hit him with a newspaper, and don't prolong the punishment. The more you praise your puppy when he is good, the more aware he will be when you punish him for something he has done wrong.

Never punish him for a mess that you've

found too late (even one minute later is too late). The puppy won't know what he is being punished for and will only be confused. Raise your voice and give punishment only at the right moment. If you yell and punish too much, the puppy will get used to it and come to expect it as part of a dog's life, and most of the time the pup will probably not understand what the punishment is for.

In all of your puppy's training, the theme is *patience* and the plan is *persistence*. Trained this way, your dog will learn faster and love you more. He will be more ready to please and obey you.

Clean up a mess right away. It's an unpleasant job, but it's part of owning a puppy.

The big breakthrough in housebreaking occurs when your dog lets you know he wants to go out.

So give your pup plenty of opportunity to go to the bathroom outside, and praise him lavishly when he does. Scold him for doing it inside only when you catch him in the act. Stick to this formula for as long as it takes. You will see gradual progress, but accidents will continue to occur until he has become fully conditioned to going outside. As he reaches middle puppyhood, from six months on, you can reduce the number of walks to four or five: morning, night, and after meals.

You must take responsibility for cleaning up the indoor messes. Keep paper towels on hand to soak up or pick up each mess, and then scrub the spot with all-purpose cleaner and water. Add a dash of vinegar to your cleaning mixture to kill any odor.

How long housebreaking takes will depend on how quickly and how carefully your dog learns to signal you that he desires to go out. Each dog has his own method: scratching at the door, a high-pitched cry, running or jumping back and forth in an attempt to get your attention, nudging you with his nose. Watch for these signals and respond to them, and praise him even more than usual when they lead to the desired results. This is the big breakthrough!

A fully housebroken dog will never mess indoors unless he is left for an entire day without a walk. But in that case, you must take the blame.

Eventually, most dogs learn the meaning of the question, "Do you want to go OUT?" They will definitely let you know if the answer is "YES!"

If your pup nips your finger while you are playing, make sure he knows that is a bad thing to do. Say "No!"

4

Puppy Games

Once a puppy gets used to his new home, he will be ready to play. Just get down on the floor with the pup and he should be eager for a good time.

During playtime you and your puppy will develop a close attachment. As you play, you will be able to show him that you are both gentle and strong. He will develop greater respect for you.

One important thing the puppy must

Most dogs will learn to fetch a stick or ball and return it to you. But be patient. Don't chase after him if he does not bring the stick right back to you.

learn about play is that biting is not part of the game. During the excitement and enthusiasm of play, a puppy will often dig its sharp little teeth into your hand or arm. Don't allow that. When he does nip you, give him a firm but gentle smack across his nose and loudly say "NO!" You don't want to hurt the pup, just startle him and make him realize that you mean business. Do exactly the same thing every time he really tries to close those teeth on you. After a while, you will notice that he puts his teeth on you only with the greatest care. You have taught him how far he can go.

Puppies love some games so much that they will play them over and over again. One of these games is to chase and, sometimes, to return a ball. A puppy can play this game for a long time. Why he plays this game is clear: it is an expression of his hunting instinct.

When he returns to you with the ball, he may try to tease you a bit. He'll come close, but won't drop the ball. You'll reach for it, and he'll hold it tight or back away. Don't try to get it away from him. Let him come to you and drop the ball. Remember that he really wants to chase it again,

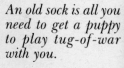

An old sock is all you need to get a puppy to play tug-of-war with you.

so be patient. A puppy will quickly lose interest in a ball without someone to toss it.

Another favorite puppy game is tug-of-war. A few rags knotted tightly together into a "rope" or just an old sock is all you need. This game can occupy some dogs in much the same way that chasing a ball can. The puppy will pull and pull, shake its head back and forth, brace its feet, and growl playfully. This is good exercise and good fun.

There is one game puppies want to play that you should not play. It is not good to chase a puppy. If you do, it will be difficult for you to teach your dog to come to you. It is all right for him to chase you, but always resist the temptation to chase him. If he invites a chase, just wait for him to come to you. Once he senses that you are not interested, he'll give up such efforts.

Besides being fun, playing with your pup will help you teach him some basic rules of behavior and loyalty. He will begin to understand who is boss and what is allowed and what is not. The next chapter talks about other rules that your puppy must learn.

Most dogs can't resist the contents of a garbage pail.

5

Building Good Puppy Habits

Many people who own puppies are so in love with them that they are reluctant to say "no" when it is needed. Your puppy will do whatever you let him do. You may think that he is just too cute to discipline. But when he grows up, it will no longer be cute when your puppy is a nuisance or behaves badly.

You should start to change bad puppy habits during the very first days. Raiding the garbage pail, lounging on chairs and couches, chewing on shoes and clothing, gnawing on table legs, stealing food, or jumping up on people are all undesirable. Some bad habits are more tolerable than others, but there is no reason to put up with any of them.

Raiding the garbage pail is one of the hardest things to teach a dog not to do, especially when the aroma of some delicious food scraps teases his nostrils. The best strategy is to not tempt the puppy. Keep the garbage pail where he can't get at it. Later, after you have broken the puppy's other bad habits, you can put the garbage pail back where it was. Then, if your dog goes into it and you catch him in the act, grab the fur on the back of his neck, give it a good shake, and say "NO" in your voice of authority.

Most people, especially parents, do not appreciate a dog who lies on furniture. The problem is that dogs love to get comfortable on something soft, and they will do just that until shown otherwise. When you catch your pup up on the furniture, grab his neck fur and throw him off. Say "GET DOWN." Do this every time you catch him, even when you're in a generous or forgiving mood. Being inconsistent will only confuse your dog about what your policy is. A nice compromise gesture is to get your dog a soft bed of his own where he can get comfortable.

Chewing or gnawing on shoes, furniture, or any other thing you value is another "NO," accompanied by a light but firm slap on the nose. It

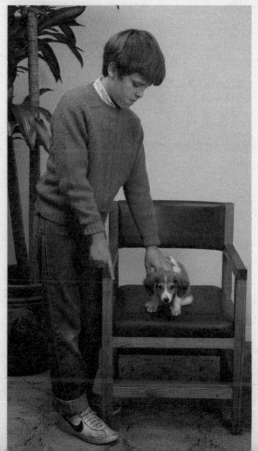

It is best to always order your puppy down from furniture. It will confuse him if you sometimes let him stay but then order him down at other times.

is a fact, however, that dogs love to gnaw and chew. So give them something more delicious than a shoe, like the rawhide bones sold in pet stores. These bones should satisfy your dog's urge to chew. But it is still a good idea to keep shoes out of your dog's reach.

This bull mastiff gets disciplined when he is bad, but he also knows when he is good.

Another bad dog habit is jumping up on people to greet them. This bothers most people and is not considered good behavior, even if the dog is only trying to be friendly. Always push the dog right back down when he jumps up, and ask that others do the same. But don't spurn his affection. Whenever possible, bend down to pet him before he has the chance to jump up. If he continues to jump up, push him down harder than you have been doing and say "DOWN" even more loudly and firmly.

Next on the bad habit list is stealing food. A dog must learn that food on a counter, a table, or in someone's hand is not for him. Never let your dog steal food. Never let him finish food he has grabbed. Take it from him right away! If you catch him in the act, take the food away, say "NO" and give him a firm slap on his nose.

Finally, it bears repeating that puppies must learn that they cannot use their teeth on people. They must not bite. Never make an exception, even when it seems to happen by mistake. Biting is best answered by the strongest "NO" and the firmest slap.

Discipline can wear out both you and your dog if you lose patience and overdo it. Remember to discipline your puppy only at the time he does something bad. Don't do it even a minute later, and only say one firm "NO" or "GET DOWN" accompanied with one firm shake or slap on the nose, if needed. Do this each time it is necessary. Be consistent, and the message will eventually get across. Your dog will remember the things that lead to a negative reaction on your part. He will also remember the good behavior that pleases you.

Much of your success in teaching your dog to behave properly depends on the affection and praise you give him when he is good. Also, don't let too many minutes go by after discipline before letting your dog know that you love him. Give him a good rub and a pat on the head. He will appreciate that.

6

Grooming and Bathing

Get your puppy accustomed to being combed and brushed regularly. You need to do this once or twice a week, depending on your dog's type of fur. Grooming is especially important for dogs with long hair.

At first, don't expect much cooperation from your puppy. Be ready to practice a little deception. When the dog tries to squirm, bounce, and get away, don't discipline him. Just act as though you understand how tough it is to be

Gently introduce your dog to brushing while he's young.

You will need a brush and comb suited to your dog's coat.

brushed. Speak lovingly to your dog to calm him, and pet him gently. Then work the brush or comb right into the rhythm of your petting.

Don't give in to the urge to be rough. Just continue to talk calmly to your dog and to stroke him. Make him feel as though he is noble and courageous and the most outstanding dog in the whole world. Just keep combing and brushing. Stop to soothe the brave fellow whenever you might hit a snag that pulls and hurts him.

The early attempts at grooming might seem unpleasant to the dog, so have someone help you hold him still. Have this person take part in your efforts to calm the dog with sympathy and praise.

You might think, "Why should I be nice to him if he won't obey me?" But try to understand that the dog does not know what brushing is all about. He just knows it feels strange, and it might sometimes be painful. Your job is not to convince the dog that he has to sit there and take

31

it. Your job is to get him to believe that nothing bad is happening and that he is strong and noble.

If you do all of these things properly, the dog will accept being brushed and will be thankful to you for seeing him gently through the grooming process.

Clipping the dog's toenails is an even more difficult job than brushing. Like the nails on your fingers and toes, a dog's toenails grow. How do you know when the nails need clipping? You will hear them making a racket as they click away on bare floors. Clipping a dog's nails is a job that requires the help of someone a little older than you. You can buy special nail clippers for dogs in a pet store. If the dog is uncooperative, you must ask the vet or a professional groomer to do it.

Occasionally, a puppy or grown dog will need a bath. How do you know when? He will have a bad smell or, if he has white or light-colored fur, you will notice when his coat is dirty.

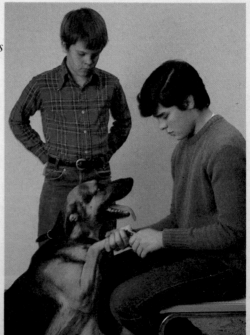

Clipping your dog's nails is a job for someone older.

Dogs react in many different ways to water. Some dogs hate it. Some love to swim in it. Some wait for the moment that the garden hose comes on because they love to dodge the squirting water. Others hide under the car.

However a dog feels about water in general, a bath probably will not be high on his list of fun things to do. At best, your dog will sit there and take it. At worst, he will act like you are trying to hurt him. Giving your dog a bath is a two-person job, and both people should be prepared to get soaked.

Use dog shampoo, baby shampoo, or a mild unperfumed soap to bathe your dog. The bathtub is as good a place as any for large dogs, and a small tub or sink will work with small dogs.

You can give a bath to a small dog right in a small tub or sink.

After a bath, make sure that you dry your dog thoroughly with a towel.

33

Giving this powerful English bulldog a bath might be a bit more of a challenge.

In warm weather a hose in the back yard will also work. Tie your dog to his leash, and have your helper hold the leash. Get the dog wet. Soap up his entire coat, carefully avoiding his eyes and ears. Then rinse him off with the hose, or pour water over him from a container. Make sure the rinse water is clean, and continue rinsing until all the soap is all out of his coat.

After you finish, let the dog shake himself off a few times. Then step in with a towel and rub him dry. Do a good job with the towel, or your dog will finish the job either on the rug, against the furniture, or outside in a flower bed.

If you give your dog a bath in cold weather, make sure that he is absolutely dry before you let him outside.

7

Training

Even though you will be busy housebreaking your puppy and keeping him out of trouble, you can begin to teach him basic commands at any time. You don't have to start immediately, but by the time your dog is six months old, he should obey your commands. At that age, he will be getting less wild and he should be more willing to cooperate.

The five things that all dogs should learn to do on command are: sit, stay, come, lie down, and heel. Heel means to walk at your side on a leash. Most professional dog trainers recommend that all of these things be taught with the dog on a leash.

Training a dog requires that you have a positive and willing attitude. Your dog will be very sensitive not only to what you say, but also to how you feel. The training sessions themselves should be short—not much longer than fifteen minutes, because that is about the length of a dog's atten-

A slip collar, used properly, makes the training of your dog a much easier job.

tion span. You should hold at least one session each day once serious training begins.

The first step in every training session is to put the chain slip collar on your dog correctly. This collar is designed to tighten quickly around the dog's neck when you jerk back firmly on the leash. This "corrective jerk" instantly changes the position and the movement of your dog. As soon as the dog stops fighting your control, the slip collar will relax and will once again hang loosely around the neck. The chain should run across the top of the dog's neck and connect with the leash on the side of the dog where you are standing. This is the only correct position. Otherwise the slip collar will not relax when the dog stops pulling, which defeats its purpose.

Teaching a dog to sit is the most basic command and the easiest one for a dog to learn. Stand next to him. With one hand, push down on

Teach your dog to sit by pushing down on his rear as you say the command "sit!"

Teach your dog the command "stay." If he starts to get up, put your hand under his chin and push up firmly.

To teach your dog to come to you, say "come," as you pat the side of your leg.

his rear as you say "SIT" in a clear, distinctive voice. As you push, hold the leash in the other hand and pull up lightly so that the chain slip collar tightens. This steadies your dog's head and neck. For a very restless dog, jerk up more firmly on the leash to achieve greater control.

Even though you have provided the push and pull, say "GOOD DOG" once he is sitting. Repeat this process over and over, always offering praise. The dog will soon learn what he is supposed to do, but he may not do it every time until he has been rehearsed daily for several weeks.

Once your dog responds to "SIT," try to keep him in that position. Hold your hand under his chin and say "STAY." Back off a few feet. He will get up. Tell him to "SIT" again. Grab his chin and say "STAY." Keep within reach of the chin so that when he attempts to get up again you can push his chin up and say "STAY" again. This is harder for him to learn than "SIT," but it involves the same process. You are training your dog to recognize and respond to a command that goes against his puppy urge to do as he pleases. **37**

Be patient. Offer praise at every opportunity. And don't confuse your dog with long sentences. Stick to a single word command when possible.

Once your dog learns to "STAY" when you walk away, the next logical step is to teach him to "COME." Since he is probably not all that excited about having to "STAY," he will be glad to "COME" at your command. Clap your hands together for encouragement. Praise and pet him when he gets to you. Then run him through the whole series, over and over, until he will "SIT," "STAY," and "COME" perfectly on command.

Next is the command to "LIE DOWN." This can be tricky. As you push your dog down into a lying position, he will be a little confused and will resist. Say the command "LIE DOWN" clearly and push him down. Then, as always, praise him and pet him for his great courage and obedience. Teaching your dog to "LIE DOWN" is

Push your dog down into a lying position and say "lie down."

important. There will be times—like when company arrives at your home—when lying down is the exact position you will want him in. Many trainers insist that for this command you should use the word "DOWN," to keep things simple. Many dog owners prefer to use "LIE DOWN," however, because the command "DOWN" is conveniently and commonly used for telling a dog to get down when it jumps up on someone with its front paws or when it lounges on a chair or couch.

With the slip collar fitted correctly on your dog, you can begin to teach him to "HEEL"—to walk at your side on a leash. Hold the leash six to twelve inches from the collar and begin to walk. When the dog pulls ahead or lags behind, say "HEEL" in your voice of authority and jerk firmly on the leash so that it tightens around the dog's neck and pulls him back into position.

Your dog will begin to realize that he can walk comfortably only when he is right at your

To teach your dog to walk at your side, jerk firmly on the leash when he moves away from you, and say the command "heel."

Whenever your dog makes even slight progress, give him plenty of praise.

side. Walk normally at first, but as he progresses get him used to fast walking and slow running as well. Make turns to the left and right. Use the command "HEEL" each time you must jerk on the leash. If the slip collar doesn't loosen when your dog heels correctly, check again to make sure that the collar is on properly.

There is never any reason to punish or yell at your dog while he is learning "HEEL" or any other command. Some dogs learn more quickly than others. If you are patient and calm and stick to it, giving a consistent lesson each day, your dog will do the best he can.

Remember to pet and praise your dog with each small success and whenever else he seems to need it. This will calm him and reassure him that you love him and that his efforts to please you are appreciated.

8

Watching Your Dog's Health

Your dog cannot talk to you. He can't come over to you and say, "Gee, I don't feel well today, maybe you should take me to the vet." In fact, he might be very sick without complaining at all. That is why you have to keep an eye on him for signs of illness.

Take your dog for a yearly visit to the vet, for booster shots and a general checkup. At the time of the visit, the vet should be able to tell you if your dog has any problems.

The signs of ill health that you should watch for in your dog are a lack of energy, a bad smell, an unusual amount of scratching, a lot of chewing and scratching at one spot on his body, weight loss, continuous vomiting over the course of a day, continuous diarrhea for a period of two days, or blood in his droppings or urine.

Make sure that your dog is healthy. Check his coat for fleas, ticks, or skin problems.

41

Take your dog right to the vet if any of these symptoms last for more than a short time. If your dog scratches or chews a lot, carefully examine his coat and skin. You might find fleas, a sore, or a patch of dried skin. If he has a bad smell, examine the dog's ears. They often have a bad odor when something is wrong. Not responding to you can be a sign of something serious. If your dog does not even want to move, call the vet immediately.

The vet will probably inoculate (give a shot to) your dog against heart worm whether you ask him to or not. But to be certain, ask the vet to do it.

Your job, as caretaker for your pup, is to catch potential health problems before they become serious and to see that they are taken care of. Work with your parents and the vet to make sure that your dog stays healthy and happy.

All dogs should get an annual check-up from a veterinarian.

9

When Your Dog Has Puppies

Both male and female dogs reach mating age at around eight months. When males reach this age, they become more aggressive and tend to roam away from home if they can. They also tend to fight with other male dogs.

Female dogs at this age come into "heat" and attract male dogs. This happens every six months or so and lasts for about three weeks. If you do intend to let a female dog have puppies, it is still best to keep her from mating the first time she comes into season. She probably needs more time to grow up in order to be a good mother.

To prevent a female dog in season from mating, you must keep her away from males. After her first time in heat, you can have her "spayed" so that she cannot have puppies, if that is your choice. The vet performs an operation on her that is a simple, routine procedure and will not change her personality. After a female dog is spayed she will not come into heat and will not attract male dogs.

A male dog can be "neutered" so that he does not have the powerful instinct to mate. Let the vet decide when the operation should be performed (a year or older is the usual time).

If you decide to let a female dog have 43

puppies, then you are responsible for helping her raise the pups. And you must find homes for the pups when they are old enough to leave their mother.

It takes about nine weeks from the time of mating for puppies to be born. The size of litters ranges from two pups to about ten, averaging around six or seven. Some puppies from a litter may not survive their first few weeks. They may have been hurt during birth or something may have affected their development.

Provide the mother-to-be with a comfortable place to give birth, even though she is just as likely to find her own "nest" as to accept the one you arrange. Give her enough privacy to feel comfortable, but do not leave her all alone.

This West Highland white terrier, called a "Westie" for short, is friendly and affectionate. A change in temperament would be a sign of illness that a vet should investigate.

Three white puppies make a formidable team. "The Polar Bears" would be a good nickname for them.

After the puppies are born, let the mother do things her way. When the pups grow past the helpless stage, at about four weeks, and their eyes open, you can handle them more frequently. Handling them at an early stage begins the important process of getting them used to people.

When the puppies are six weeks old, put notices on bulletin boards or in your local newspaper that you have puppies to sell or give away. Have the pups weaned—switched from their mother's milk to puppy food—and ready to be picked up by new owners at around eight weeks.

Without being impolite, ask a few honest questions of the people who come for puppies. Try to find out if they understand what their responsibilities are going to be. You may decide to explain some of these responsibilities to them. 45

10

A Good Dog and a Good Pet

When your dog is full-grown and well-trained, he will be a source of pride to you. He will obey your commands with little hesitation. He will always come when you call. He will be at your side when you need his companionship.

As he grows older you will get to know your dog's "personality," his likes and dislikes, and his needs. Your dog, in turn, will learn what pleases you. He will come to you for affection and reassurance that he is, in fact, *your* dog.

Never forget to show your dog that you appreciate him.

Never take him for granted. Never forget to show your appreciation. Try as hard as you can to always walk your dog on time, feed him every day, and make sure that he gets enough exercise. Encourage your dog to get to know other people and encourage other people to be friendly to your dog.

Whenever possible, take your dog to a large open field or any rural setting where he can run free. Remember to keep him close to you, under control, whenever other dogs are around or you are ready to cross a street or road.

In the end, all of your patience and effort will pay off. Your dog's loyalty and obedience and your own affection for him will form a strong bond of friendship between the the two of you.

INDEX